Content

An Ancient Information Highway

Between about 60 B.C. and the late A.D. 1400s, a flourishing trade was conducted over the Silk Road, which stretched from eastern China to the **Middle East**. The name "Silk Road" is somewhat misleading. The "road" was actually a system of different routes. Europe was also part of the trade network, linked to the Middle East and the Silk Road by a second system of routes.

Although silk was highly prized, it was not the only valuable item carried along the Silk Road. China also exported such things as medicinal herbs, oranges, tea, gunpowder, compasses, furs, carved jade, bronze objects, **lacquerware**, and other luxury goods to the Middle East. China used the Silk Road to import items such as gold, silver, glassware, ivory, wool rugs, nuts, peaches, cucumbers, onions, cotton, and horses.

Trade goods were not the only things that were transported along the Silk Road. Traders and travelers spread foods, **technologies**, ideas, and religions to places far away from their original homes. For example, Chinese inventions such as paper, printing, fireworks, and noodles were introduced into Europe and the Middle East by Silk Road traders and travelers. Merchants from India introduced the religion of Buddhism into China. The Silk Road's greatest importance lies in its role in this exchange of ideas and information, which transformed the civilizations of Asia, the Middle East, and Europe.

This is a picture of the Buddhist temple located in the Norbulingka Institute in northern India. This temple is decorated with 1,173 images of Buddha, the founder of Buddhism.

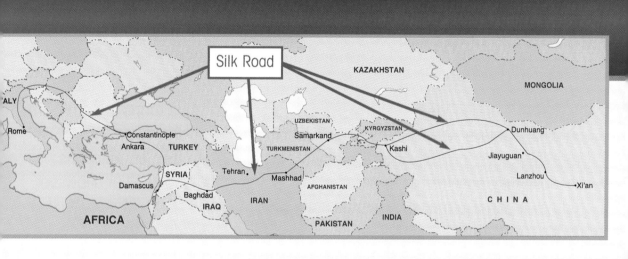

Silk Road

KAZAKHSTAN

MONGOLIA

ALY

Rome

Constantinople

Ankara TURKEY

UZBEKISTAN KYRGYZSTAN

Samarkand Dunhuang

TURKMENISTAN Kashi

SYRIA Tehran Jiayuguan

Damascus Mashhad Lanzhou

Baghdad AFGHANISTAN Xi'an

IRAQ IRAN CHINA

AFRICA PAKISTAN INDIA

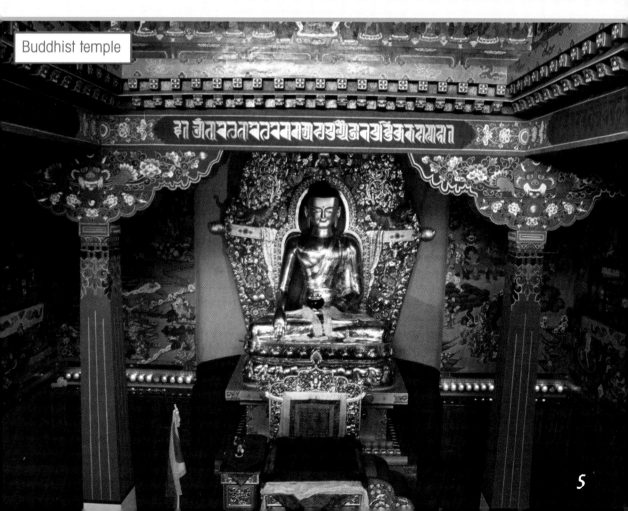

Buddhist temple

Using Maps to Learn About the Silk Road

Traders and travelers on the Silk Road did not have maps to help them on their journeys. Travelers often found their way by asking others how to get from one place to another. Most traders did not have to ask for directions because they traveled routes with which they were already familiar. However, today we can use maps to help us learn about the Silk Road. Maps can show us the routes that made up the Silk Road. They can show us the cities through which traders and travelers passed and the mountains, deserts, and rivers they had to cross.

Maps can also show us the almost 4,000 miles covered by the Silk Road. To measure distances on a map, we use the map scale. The map scale shows us how to use distances on the map to figure out actual distances. Different maps use different scales. The scale used on a map is usually shown in one of the map's corners.

The scale on a map is an indicator of the relationship between distances on the map and the corresponding actual distances. For example, suppose you have a map with a scale of 1 inch = 100 miles. To find the actual distance between 2 cities that are 3 inches apart on the map, you would multiply 100 miles by 3 to get 300 miles.

$$\begin{array}{r} 100 \text{ miles per inch} \\ \times\ 3 \text{ inches} \\ \hline 300 \text{ actual miles} \end{array}$$

Three inches on a map with a scale of 1 inch = 100 miles would equal 300 actual miles.

desert hills surrounding Silk Road

section of Silk Road in northern Iran

Traders and travelers on the Silk Road passed through difficult and often dangerous landscapes, including deserts, rugged mountains, and vast grasslands.

section of Silk Road in Pakistan

7

Let's use the scale on the map shown below to measure the distance along the Silk Road from its starting point in Xi'an (SHE-AN), China, to Constantinople, which today is called Istanbul, Turkey. First, use a ruler to measure the distance on the map. Since the road twists and turns, you can't just measure in a straight line from Xi'an to Constantinople. You have to measure short sections of the route, trying to follow the curves as closely as possible. Write down the total number of inches for the distance.

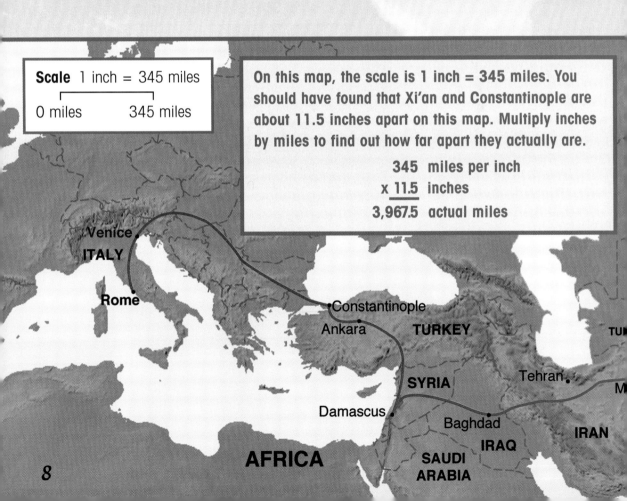

Scale 1 inch = 345 miles

0 miles   345 miles

On this map, the scale is 1 inch = 345 miles. You should have found that Xi'an and Constantinople are about 11.5 inches apart on this map. Multiply inches by miles to find out how far apart they actually are.

345 miles per inch
x 11.5 inches
3,967.5 actual miles

Venice
ITALY

Rome

Constantinople
Ankara   TURKEY   TU

SYRIA   Tehran   M

Damascus
Baghdad   IRAN
IRAQ
AFRICA   SAUDI
ARABIA

Now consult the scale, which is in the upper lefthand corner of the map. It says that 1 inch = 345 miles. To find the actual distance between Constantinople and Xi'an, multiply the number of inches by the number of miles each inch represents.

The distance from the beginning point of the Silk Road in Xi'an, China, to Constantinople is almost 4,000 miles. Imagine making a journey that long, across deserts and through mountains, with no means of travel other than your own feet and perhaps a horse for part of the journey!

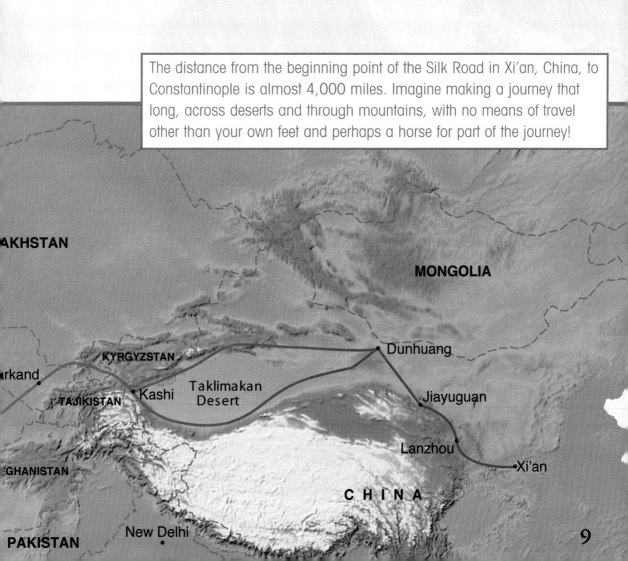

AKHSTAN

MONGOLIA

Dunhuang

KYRGYZSTAN

rkand

Kashi   Taklimakan
           Desert   Jiayuguan

TAJIKISTAN

Lanzhou

GHANISTAN   •Xi'an

CHINA

New Delhi

PAKISTAN   9

The Early History of the Silk Road

The Silk Road originated about 2,500 years ago, made possible by the **domestication** of camels. Traders needed strong animals to carry their goods. Horses, which needed food and water daily, could not cross the deserts of central Asia. The traders could not carry water with them, and there were no dependable sources of water along the way. However, camels could cross the deserts easily, since they could go for long periods without food or water. **Caravans** of camels traveled between the **oasis** trading cities along the Silk Road.

Few traders traveled the entire length of the Silk Road. Most caravan drivers and their camels traveled back and forth on one section of the road. For example, one trader might cover the section from Xi'an, at the eastern end of the Silk Road, to Lanzhou (LAHN-JOH), a city on the Yellow River. In ancient times, Lanzhou was an important government center. A palace from this time still exists. Lanzhou was also known as the "Gold City" after gold was discovered there. Use the map on page 11 to find the distance between Xi'an and Lanzhou.

Taklimakan Desert

The Taklimakan Desert in northwest China is the second largest desert in the world. A section of the Silk Road passed along the edge of this desolate region. Without camels, traders and travelers would not have been able to make the journey.

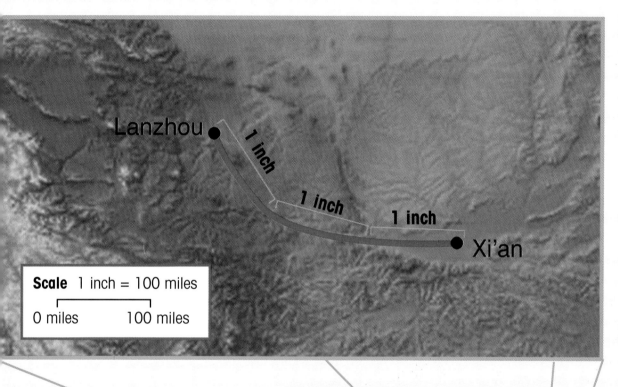

Lanzhou

1 inch

1 inch

1 inch

Xi'an

Scale 1 inch = 100 miles

0 miles   100 miles

100   miles per inch

x   3   inches
_____
300   actual miles

The distance from Xi'an to
Lanzhou along the Silk Road
was about 300 miles.

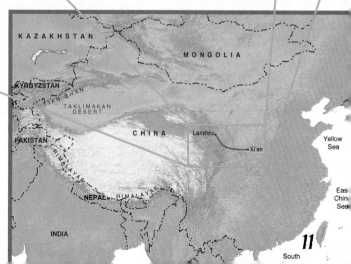

Traders would pick up silk and other goods in Xi'an to take to Lanzhou. Silk was highly valued in China at the time. In addition to being used for clothes, it was used for things such as musical instruments, fishing line, and paper.

In Lanzhou, traders could exchange the silk and other goods from Xi'an for goods from southern Asia and the Middle East. Another trader might take the silk and other goods from Lanzhou to the next city. The first trader would return to Xi'an, where he would trade his newly acquired goods for more silk and other Chinese goods, and the process would begin again.

In 221 B.C., China's first emperor made the ancient city of Xi'an his capital. These life-size clay statues come from the emperor's tomb in Xi'an.

Lanzhou became an important hub on the Silk Road. Traders from different cultures met there to trade goods. Goods from the Middle East reached Lanzhou on the main east-west passage of the Silk Road. Goods from southern Asia traveled to Lanzhou along a second route, which ran southwest to the Bay of Bengal in the Northern Indian Ocean.

The city of Lanzhou is on the Yellow River. Today, Lanzhou is an important industrial and cultural center.

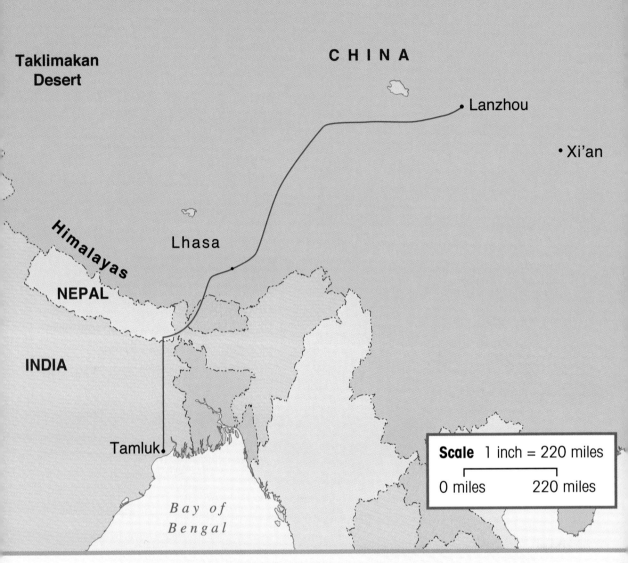

Scale 1 inch = 220 miles

0 miles   220 miles

Lanzhou to Lhasa	Lhasa to Tamluk
220 miles per inch x 3.5 inches 770 actual miles	220 miles per inch x 2.25 inches 495 actual miles
The distance from Lanzhou to Lhasa along the Silk Road was about 770 miles.	The distance from Lhasa to Tamluk along the Silk Road was about 495 miles.

Two important trading cities located on the southwest route were Lhasa (LAH-suh), in the region of China known as Tibet, and Tamluk (tuhm-LUK), near Calcutta, India. What distance would a trader have traveled on the Silk Road between Lanzhou and Lhasa? What distance would a trader have traveled on the Silk Road between Lhasa and Tamluk? We can use the scale on the map on page 14 to find the answers.

The difficult route between Lanzhou and Tamluk on the Bay of Bengal required travelers to cross the great Himalaya mountain system. Most of the mountain passes that cross the Himalayas are 15,000 to 16,000 feet above sea level and are covered with snow from November until May. This often made the passes difficult or impossible to cross. As a result, the route between Lanzhou and Tamluk was not heavily traveled.

The Himalaya mountain system is 1,500 miles long and has the tallest mountains in the world. Despite such an overwhelming obstacle, some Chinese traders still braved the Himalayas to trade goods in India.

The First Great Age

By 60 B.C., China's ruling Han **dynasty** was powerful enough to protect Silk Road traders and travelers from attacks by outlaws and by China's enemies. Trade flourished, and Chinese authorities began to conduct official government trade on the Silk Road.

The Chinese government used the Silk Road to obtain more horses for its army. At the time, the world's best horses were believed to come from the Fergana (fir-guh-NAH) Valley, which lies just west of the Tian Shan (TYEN SHAHN) mountains in far western China. Government agents, protected by soldiers, set out from Xi'an to make the long journey to the Fergana Valley. Use this map to find out how far they traveled. Notice that the Silk Road divided into two branches at Dunhuang (DUN-HWANG), one passing to the north of the Taklimakan Desert and one to the south. The two branches rejoined at Kashi (KAH-SHIH). Measure the northern route from Xi'an first. Remember to measure it in short sections, following its curves as closely as possible.

This 2-foot-tall clay figure, created during the Han dynasty, probably comes from the tomb of a military leader. The horse is similar to those the Chinese government obtained from the Fergana Valley.

16

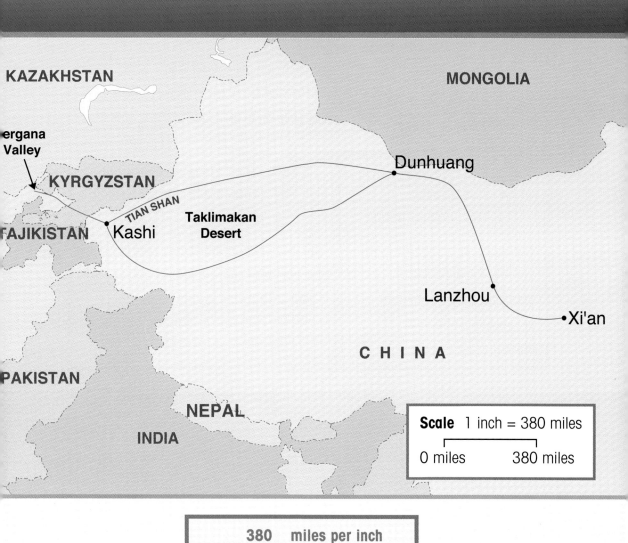

KAZAKHSTAN

MONGOLIA

Fergana
Valley

KYRGYZSTAN

Dunhuang

TIAN SHAN

TAJIKISTAN   Kashi

Taklimakan
Desert

Lanzhou

Xi'an

CHINA

PAKISTAN

NEPAL

INDIA

Scale 1 inch = 380 miles

0 miles   380 miles

$$\begin{array}{r} 380 \\ \times\ 6.5 \\ \hline 2{,}470 \end{array} \quad \begin{array}{l} \text{miles per inch} \\ \text{inches} \\ \text{actual miles} \end{array}$$

The distance between Xi'an and
the Fergana Valley along the
northern route of the Silk Road
was about 2,470 miles.

Now measure the southern route from Xi'an to the Fergana Valley shown on page 17. What was the difference in length between the 2 routes? Which route do you think the government caravans used?

```
    380   miles per inch
  x 7.25  inches
  2,755   actual miles
```

The distance between Xi'an and the Fergana Valley along the southern route of the Silk Road was about 2,755 miles.

```
  2,755  miles along southern route
– 2,470  miles along northern route
    285  miles
```

The government caravans used the northern route because it was about 285 miles shorter than the southern route.

By this time, silk had become a form of currency in China. It was widely desired because it is one of the strongest natural materials. It is even stronger than thread made of steel! Chinese farmers made silk by unwinding the cocoons made by silkworms. They combined many of the slender threads into a single, thicker thread. The Chinese government had a lot of silk because the farmers who collected it from silkworms used it to pay their taxes. The government caravans carried silk to trade for the horses.

Once the government caravans had traded their silk for horses in the Fergana Valley, they immediately began the return trip. The camels carried the food and water supply for the horses during the journey around the Taklimakan Desert. In spite of these provisions, horses often died from the harsh conditions on the return trip.

After the Han dynasty ended in A.D. 220, China broke apart into 3 kingdoms. This period is known as the age of the Northern and Southern Dynasties. For almost 4 centuries, there was no central Chinese government to protect the Silk Road. Nevertheless, trade flourished because the rulers of the 3 kingdoms encouraged trade and cultural exchange with other civilizations. New customs, unfamiliar goods, and new religions soon reached China.

Silk, shown in the picture here, quickly became popular with Romans when they first encountered it around 55 B.C. They admired its beauty and softness.

In the centuries following the Han dynasty, Buddhism became an important religion in China. Buddhism was founded in India in the 500s or 400s B.C. It teaches that suffering in the world can be overcome by people leading positive, moral lives. Buddhists also believe that they will be reborn after death.

Buddhism was introduced into China by way of the Silk Road and other trade routes. It first reached China during the Han dynasty, but its greatest growth in China happened after the Han dynasty. Many Buddhist **monasteries** were built, and millions of peasants adopted Buddhism as their religion.

Just as the Silk Road brought Buddhism into China, it allowed for the spread of the ancient Chinese **philosophy** and religion known as Taoism (TAU-ih-zuhm) into central Asia. Taoism is a way of thinking and living simply, in harmony with nature. By doing this, Taoists believe they may achieve long life and good fortune.

During this period, Christianity was also introduced into China, as was a Middle Eastern religion called Manichaeism (MA-nuh-kee-ih-zuhm). Manichaeism was established by the Persian prophet Mani in the A.D. 200s. It taught that life consisted of a struggle between the forces of good and evil. It also taught that the physical world itself was evil.

In A.D. 366, a Buddhist monk carved a temple into cliffs near the Silk Road city of Dunhuang. Hundreds more were carved over the next 1,000 years. Today, they are called the Mogao caves. Many of the 492 caves feature murals, statues, and other religious objects.

inside a Mogao cave

Mogao caves

21

The Second Great Age

The second great age of the Silk Road began in A.D. 586, when China was reunited as a single empire under the Sui (SWEE) dynasty. The second age continued under the Tang dynasty, which followed the Sui dynasty in A.D. 618. The powerful Tang rulers once again established government protection of the Silk Road. Their control extended from Xi'an to the mountainous region known as the Pamirs (puh-MIRZ), in what is today Tajikistan. Use the map on page 23 to measure how many miles of the Silk Road were protected by the Tang rulers. Measure the northern route of the Silk Road.

> 290   miles per inch
> x 7.5   inches
> 2,175   actual miles
>
> **The Tang rulers protected about 2,175 miles along the northern route of the Silk Road between Xi'an and the eastern border of modern-day Tajikistan.**

Tang rulers encouraged the flow of new goods and ideas into China. Silk Road trade introduced new types of musical instruments, new clothing styles, and even chairs, which replaced traditional Chinese floor mats. The sport of **polo** was also introduced by way of the Silk Road.

MONGOLIA

Dunhuang

KYRGYZSTAN

Kashi

JIKISTAN

KISTAN

CHINA

•Xi'an

NEPAL

INDIA

Scale 1 inch = 290 miles

0 miles   290 miles

This wall painting from a Tang dynasty tomb shows men playing polo. Polo was probably invented in Persia—modern-day Iran— more than 2,000 years ago.

23

KAZAKHSTAN

UZBEKISTAN

Tashkent

KYRGYZSTAN

TIAN SHAN

TAJIKISTAN

Taklimakan Desert

CHINA

PAKISTAN

AFGHANISTAN

The battle near Tashkent had important—though unexpected—consequences for the Middle East and Europe. The Arab army captured Chinese papermakers at the battle of the Talas River, and as a result, knowledge of how to make paper spread to the Middle East. Eventually, the knowledge also spread to Europe. This picture shows the process of papermaking.

The second great age of the Silk Road ended around A.D. 751. That year, Arab soldiers defeated soldiers of the Tang dynasty in a great battle on the Talas River near the city of Tashkent (tash-KENT), in what is today the central Asian nation of Uzbekistan. After that, Tang rulers were not able to protect traders and travelers on the western portion of the Silk Road.

The Chinese were defeated in part because the battle took place so far from Xi'an that it was difficult to get supplies to the soldiers. You've already measured the distance from Xi'an to the eastern border of Tajikistan on page 22. Use the map on page 24 to measure the distance from the eastern border of Tajikistan to Tashkent, then add the 2 distances to find out how far supplies had to travel to reach the Chinese soldiers.

4 5 miles per inch x 1.5 inches ————— 67.5 actual miles The distance between the eastern border of Tajikistan and Tashkent along the Silk Road was about 67.5 miles.	2,175.0 miles + 67.5 miles ————— 2,242.5 miles The total distance from Xi'an to Tashkent along the Silk Road was about 2,242.5 miles.

The Last Great Age

The last great age of the Silk Road took place in the 1200s and 1300s, when the Mongols ruled China. The Mongols came from the **steppes** of central Asia, a region now called Mongolia. The Mongols were fierce warriors who destroyed many of the oasis cities on the Silk Road during their battles with the Chinese. Nevertheless, they promoted trade with other cultures, and the Silk Road flourished under their rule.

The earliest European visitors to the Mongol Empire were probably Catholic **friars** who reached Mongolia in the early 1200s. The first Europeans to reach the Mongol court in Beijing (BAY-JING) were traders from northern Europe who arrived in 1261. The French king and Catholic pope also sent ambassadors to the Mongol ruler.

One of the most famous journeys made on the Silk Road took place during the reign of Mongol leader Kublai Khan (KOO-bluh KAHN). A young Italian man named Marco Polo traveled to the court of Kublai Khan with his father and uncle when he was just 17 years old. The Polos were merchants from Venice, an important port and commercial city in northern Italy. In 1271, they set out on a $3\frac{1}{2}$-year journey to the Mongol court. They remained there for 17 years before starting the long journey home. After returning to Venice in 1295, Marco Polo wrote a book about his travels, which quickly became famous. In his book, Marco Polo described such things as the trade practices, manufacturing methods, and marriage customs of the regions he traveled through. He also described the strange new plants and animals he saw on his journey.

This small painting of Marco Polo on his journey
through Asia comes from a copy of his book made
in the early 1400s. The artist, who had never been
to Asia, painted European trees, people, and clothes.

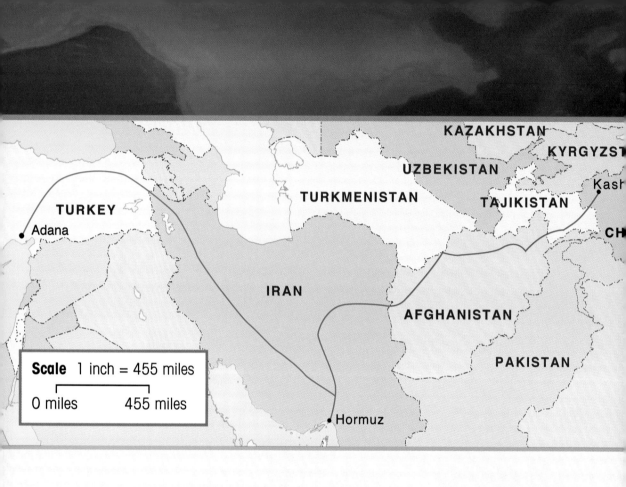

Scale 1 inch = 455 miles

0 miles   455 miles

This map shows the route the Polos followed through the Middle East. If you compare it with the map shown on pages 8 and 9, you'll see that it is different from—and longer than—the path usually followed by Silk Road travelers. Use the map on pages 8 and 9 to measure the distance from Damascus to Kashi along the Silk Road. Then use the map above to measure the overland portion of the Polos' journey from Adana on the southern coast of Turkey to Kashi. How much longer was the route followed by the Polos?

```
  345  miles per inch          455  miles per inch
x   5  inches               x 9.25  inches
-----                       ------
1,725  actual miles         4,208.75  actual miles
```

The distance between Damascus and Kashi along the Silk Road was about 1,725 miles.

The distance the Polos traveled from the southern coast of Turkey to Kashi was about 4,208.75 miles.

```
  4,208.75  miles
- 1,725.00  miles
----------
  2,483.75  miles
```

The route the Polos traveled was about 2,483.75 miles longer than the Silk Road between Damascus and Kashi.

Why do you think the Polos took this longer route? Marco's father and uncle had already made a trip to China in the 1260s. Perhaps they had met people along this route on that trip and wanted to see them again. This route also took the Polos to the important Persian port and commercial city of Hormuz; perhaps they hoped to acquire goods there that they might not find in other places.

The Mongols were not able to hold together their vast empire, which began to fall apart during Kublai Khan's time. In the late 1300s, a Turk ruler named Timur the Lame—or Tamerlane—tried to reestablish the empire. He conquered parts of the Middle East and central Asia and set up his capital city in Samarkand, in what is now Uzbekistan. In creating his empire, Tamerlane destroyed many oasis cities. This made it impossible to continue trade along the Silk Road. China's Ming dynasty, which came to power in 1368, did not want to do anything that might anger the Turks and Mongols, so they never tried to rebuild trade on the Silk Road. In the centuries that followed, trade between China, the Middle East, and Europe was carried out by ships.

Today, China trades many goods with other countries all over the world. Modern technology and **transportation** have made **commerce** much easier and quicker for all countries. Modern maps enable us to find out where we need to go, and how far we need to travel to get there. Without maps and map scales, trading with other countries might not be as widespread and profitable as it is today.

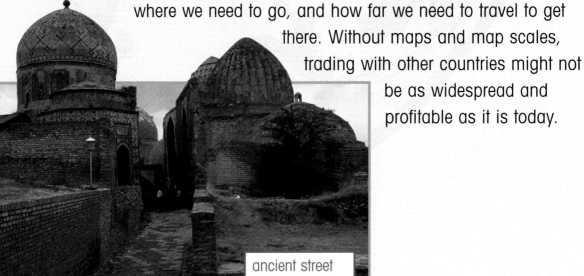

ancient street in Samarkand

Glossary

caravan (KAIR-uh-van) A group of pack animals traveling through a desert or dangerous region.

commerce (KAH-muhrs) The exchange of goods and ideas involving transportation from place to place.

domestication (duh-mess-tih-KAY-shun) The taming of a kind of animal for the purpose of performing tasks for humans.

dynasty (DYE-nuh-stee) A line of rulers from the same family.

friar (FRY-uhr) A special kind of monk who doesn't always live in a monastery.

lacquerware (LA-kuhr-wear) A decorative object, usually made of wood, that has been covered with a hard, shiny coating known as lacquer.

Middle East (MIH-duhl EEST) The countries of southwestern Asia and northern Africa.

monastery (MAH-nuh-stair-ee) A home for a community of monks.

oasis (oh-AY-suhs) An area in a desert where there is enough water for plants to grow.

philosophy (fuh-LAH-suh-fee) A system of beliefs about the meaning of life and the best way to live.

polo (POH-loh) A game played by teams of riders on horseback who use a long-handled wooden tool to knock a wooden ball through goalposts.

steppe (STEP) A vast, flat, treeless region in Asia.

technology (tek-NAH-luh-jee) An improved way of doing or making something that uses specialized processes or methods.

transportation (tranz-puhr-TAY-shun) The process of moving people and goods from one place to another.

Index